F.L.A.G.
FRAUD, LIES & GREED

F.L.A.G.
FRAUD, LIES & GREED

Cautionary Tales of How Professional Athletes

Become the Victims of Fraud

ANTONY E. GHEE

Mynd Matters Publishing

FIRST EDITION

ISBN: 978-0-9899164-6-2

Library of Congress Control Number: 2016919556

Printed in the United States of America

To Michele, Taylor and Jordan for providing me with my purpose, inspiration and motivation! To my mother (Phyllis) and grandmother (Rosa), for providing me with a strong foundation upon which to live my life and encouraging me to pursue my dreams, often in the face of seemingly insurmountable odds!

TABLE OF CONTENTS

Part III: The Schemes

Part IV: Protecting Yourself from Fraud

About the Author

Sources

Index

ACKNOWLEDGMENTS

Anyone with an interest in this book likely knows that investment fraud is a serious problem plaguing professional athletes. For that very reason, the process of researching hundreds of instances of fraud was a monumental task. Only after conducting extensive research was I able to identify the stories most suitable for this project. Indeed, there are many other stories, some well publicized and some less so, that were worthy of inclusion. However, the stories I chose to include are important for their context, detail and diversity, providing important lessons about who engages in fraudulent behavior, as well as why and how they do it. Most important, these stories provide insight into what professional athletes can and should do to protect themselves so that they do not become the next victim of fraud.

To my editor, Renita Bryant and her colleagues at Mynd Matters Publishing, who not only understood but also appreciated the message that I wanted to communicate.

To Richard Hennion, Kevin Mahn and their team at Hennion & Walsh, Inc. who has, for more than 25 years, shown a commitment to providing personalized investment services to their clients. It was over lunch (and a glass of wine) with "Rich" and Kevin that the idea for this book was born.

To Plaxico Burress, my brother in every sense of the word. You have consistently encouraged and supported me with the project and throughout this process. Having been a victim of financial misconduct during the early days of your career in the National Football League, you have provided me with invaluable insight into why professional athletes are susceptible to fraud. I have always respected how you selflessly reach back to help young players without expecting anything in return and your contribution to this effort is no different.

To Charles Smith, you are not only a friend and business partner but an inspiration! You pursue business and investing with the same intensity and competitive spirit that led you to be the third pick in the National Basketball Association's 1988 draft. I have met many professional athletes and there are few that have your hustle, drive and business acumen. I have personally witnessed you set the conditions for others to succeed, providing a legitimate platform that bridges the world of professional athletes, Wall Street and the broader business community. Professional athletes would be wise to learn from your example.

It is critical that professional athletes take serious the responsibility to secure their financial futures. Other athletes can reach back and share wisdom, while others can provide platforms for growth, but in the end, the responsibility to protect your wealth is up to you and you alone!

FOREWORD

Early in my professional career and on two separate occasions, I was the victim of financial fraud and lost considerable sums of money. As a result, I had to learn from personal experience and often wondered why no one was truly dedicated to educating professional athletes about the pitfalls and dangers of affinity fraud. Who is teaching us not only how to invest the money that WE EARN through blood, sweat and tears, but the equally important lesson of how to protect ourselves from con men and scam artists?

I urged my brother Antony to write this book because I know all too well the cost of failure in not effectively managing one's own finances. I learned how detrimental it can be to give someone the reins when their primary goal is not to build or generate wealth for a client, but to engage in fraudulent and misleading acts that result in creating wealth for themselves. Antony educates us in this book and shines a bright light on the harsh realities that professional athletes endure outside of the glitz and glamour. These are real life challenges that we face when the game is over and the cameras are turned off. Professional athletes can learn valuable lessons from my experience as well as those of their peers and predecessors. These lessons implore athletes to assume personal responsibility over their financial and business affairs so they don't fall victim to fraudulent schemes.

I am honored to write this foreword and to urge other professional athletes to take serious their responsibility to protect themselves. I hope this book provides for the next generation of professional athletes, the warnings and wisdom that I wish had been shared with me and my peers. My mom used to always say, "You can never stop the sun from shining!" Indeed, the sun is shining and the future is bright for professional athletes who read this book and embrace the responsibility to protect themselves.

Plaxico Burress
Super Bowl Champion 2007

PREFACE

In professional sports, a whistle is blown or a flag is thrown as a result of an illegal action that usually results in a stiff penalty, an ejection and sometimes a fine when a player does or says something inappropriate to an opposing player or official. Each professional sports league uses its own terminology to describe inappropriate or illegal action but it is all penalized as misconduct. In soccer, yellow and red cards are used to discipline players for misconduct. In hockey, players are sent to the penalty box. In baseball, a player may be ejected. In football, the referee tosses a yellow flag and assesses a penalty. If the misconduct is sufficiently egregious, the player will be ejected and likely fined. In basketball, the referee blows a whistle and awards the opposing team free throws or possession and depending on the nature of the misconduct, may eject the player from the game.

On Wall Street and in the world of investing, misconduct is also penalized. In theory, the severity of the misconduct should dictate the extent of the penalty. An honest mistake or simple negligence may only warrant remedial training or a fine. However, recklessness or more serious misconduct may subject the perpetrator to revocation of professional licenses, disbarment from the financial services industry or even a lengthy prison term.

Professional athletes make millions of dollars each year and financial professionals and other third-party service providers are eager to cater to their needs. This is how their two worlds intersect. In most instances, financial professionals operate with integrity and commit themselves to providing a high level of service to their clients. Unfortunately, there are some that do not. Instead, they view their potential clients as targets from whom they can extract wealth for themselves. They devise unethical schemes and engage in unnecessary and egregious misconduct designed to defraud their clients.

During the time that I was researching and writing this book, several high-profile cases of fraud and financial misconduct involving professional athletes were exposed. For example, in January 2016, NBA legend Tim Duncan sued his longtime financial advisor for $20 million, alleging that the advisor had convinced Duncan to make a series of investments without disclosing certain conflicts of interest. In addition, the lawsuit alleges that Duncan's signature was forged on at least two investment documents. On June 9, 2016, it was reported that Dallas Cowboys running back, Darren McFadden, had sued his longtime business manager for $15 million for allegedly misappropriating and mishandling money throughout his NFL career. Then in a shocking twist, on August 10, 2016, Merrill Robertson, Jr., a former NFL player, was arrested and charged along with his business partner for running a Ponzi scheme that defrauded investors of nearly $8 million. Robertson admitted that he often commingled business, personal and investor funds, stating that he used investor funds to pay for personal expenses such as his mortgage and car payments. If true, Robertson and the advisors for Duncan and McFadden are all deserving of penalties for financial misconduct and could be fined or face significant time in prison.

Financial fraud is a major issue for professional athletes. It is my hope that after reading this book, you will better understand who does it, how it happens, why it happens, and what you can do to protect yourself from becoming the next victim of fraud.

THE BIG PICTURE

The Professional Athlete's Career Lifecycle

You do not have to be a rocket scientist to be an investor. You also do not need to become an expert on every investment opportunity available. However, it is in your best interest to have a basic understanding of potential risks and rewards. Not doing so leaves your financial future to chance and you have worked too hard for too long for that to be a sensible option. It is not! Arguably, the world's greatest investor, Warren Buffet, was famously quoted saying, "never invest in a business you cannot understand." The same is true of any investment. If you do not understand the investment opportunity or its inherent risks, walk away.

Buffet's advice is true for anyone but it should truly resonate with professional athletes. The average American can suffer a financial setback during his 20's or 30's and given the traditional career trajectory, have sufficient time to rebound well in advance of retirement. According to a New York Federal Reserve Bank study, the average American will not hit their peak earning years until after they hit the half-century mark - age 50. Not so for professional athletes. Their peak earning years generally will occur well before they reach age 35. For professional athletes whose career tenure is in line with the average of 3-to-5 years, they will likely peak before they turn 30 years old.

A professional athlete's career life cycle is best viewed in three stages (Figure 1). During Stage 1, or what I call the preparatory years (which typically runs from birth until around age 22), the athlete is growing, honing his craft, and preparing himself to hopefully fulfill his dream of being drafted and given the opportunity to play his sport of choice at the professional level. Under normal circumstances, the athlete makes little to no income until he is drafted and signs his initial contract as a professional. The initial contract is sometimes referred to as the 'set-up' contract, which comes before the real money is earned in Stage 2. During Stage 2, the professional athlete is well into his career and should be acutely focused on saving and growing his wealth to prepare for his inevitable retirement. Unfortunately, it is also during Stage 2 that, for a host of reasons to be discussed later, professional athletes are most susceptible to fraud. During Stage 3, the professional athlete has retired and his investment objectives and approach should shift from growth to capital preservation.

It is critical to the professional athlete's long-term financial success that he begin financial planning early in his career. By embracing good habits early and building a team of competent and trustworthy financial professionals, the athlete can avoid many of the mistakes made by his contemporaries who will unfortunately face financial distress in retirement, if not sooner.

Figure 1 – Professional Athlete's Career Lifecycle

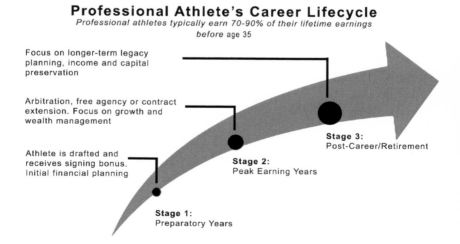

Professional Athlete's Career Lifecycle
Professional athletes typically earn 70-90% of their lifetime earnings before age 35

Focus on longer-term legacy planning, income and capital preservation

Arbitration, free agency or contract extension. Focus on growth and wealth management

Athlete is drafted and receives signing bonus. Initial financial planning

Stage 1: Preparatory Years

Stage 2: Peak Earning Years

Stage 3: Post-Career/Retirement

The Great Illusion of Financial Security

If you receive a $5 million signing bonus today, what would you do with the money? Though the dollar amounts may differ, that is the question a professional athlete must answer every time he signs a new contract or scores a big payday. Quite frankly, it is the same question each of us must answer every time we receive a paycheck. In many cases, there is an immediate urge to consume—buy a new car for dad, buy a new home for mom, take our spouse on that fantasy vacation, buy new clothes or jewelry, or make some other unnecessary purchase. Because we live in a culture of consumption, this thinking has become normalized. Unfortunately, it has also led many professional athletes to financial distress following, and sometimes during, their athletic careers. According to one source, as many as 78% of professional athletes are bankrupt within four years of retirement. While those statistics are debatable, Figure 2 is a sobering reminder that many professional athletes, despite having made millions of dollars throughout their careers, will fail to achieve financial security.

Figure 2 – Professional Athletes: Bankruptcy and Financial Distress

- Professional athletes often do not receive sound financial advice throughout their careers and ultimately face bankruptcy or serious financial stress shortly after their playing careers are over.

 80% of NFL players face bankruptcy or serious financial stress within two years of retiring

 60% of NBA players face bankruptcy or serious financial stress within five years of retiring

 MLB players file bankruptcy **4x more often** than the national average

- As a general rule, less than 10 out of every 1,000 people in the U.S. file bankruptcy every year.

There are many reasons why professional athletes experience financial difficulties or file for bankruptcy. A key reason is lack of understanding. Some athletes do not understand the limitations of their contracts and the reality that the value of the contract does not equal the amount of cash they will actually put in their pocket. For example, using my $5 million bonus scenario, some athletes may assume that by receiving that bonus, they are increasing their discretionary spending power by $5 million. Not so! In reality, that athlete is likely to only take home around $700,000 if he is lucky. Let me explain. An athlete will typically: pay about 40% in taxes, pay up to 10% to their agent depending on which sport they play, pay their attorneys and accountants for services rendered, and in many cases, choose to buy mom and dad a new car or home. After accounting for those expenses, that $5 million bonus ends up being around $700,000 in the athlete's bank account (see Figure 3). And that is before he buys a single thing for himself. Much of that what is left may go towards purchasing a new car, buying new clothes, jewelry or whatever is en vogue at the time. Given those facts, it is no surprise many athletes end up in financial straits.

FIGURE 3 – How A Typical NFL $5 Million Signing Bonus Is Blown

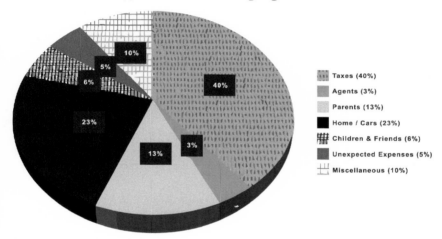

There is another important consideration. Not all professional sports contracts are guaranteed. In particular, most NFL contracts are not fully guaranteed. In contrast, the NBA, NHL, and MLB usually offer guaranteed contracts to their players. Under those conditions, it is more likely than not that the player will receive the full value of the contract. However, even in those situations, athletes must be cognizant of their tax obligations, agent commissions, the cost of third-party professional services, and importantly, their personal consumption habits. Figure 4 details the maximum commission allowed for some of the most popular professional sports leagues, as well as the average annual salary, career length and career earnings.

FIGURE 4 – Commissions, Career and Salary Averages

Sport	Maximum Commissions	Average Annual Salary	Average Career Length	Average Career Earnings
NFL	3%	$1.9 million	3.5 years	$6.7 million
NBA	4%	$5.15 million	4.8 years	$24.7 million
MLB	4%	$3.2 million	5.6 years	$17.9 million
NHL	5%	$2.4 million	5.5 years	$13.2 million
FIFA	10%	$6.7 million	8 years	$53.6 million

Note that Major League Soccer (MLS) has been excluded because earnings are negligible in comparison to other professional sports leagues.

There are a host of other reasons why professional athletes experience financial difficulties such as legal troubles, divorce, child support and childcare payments, and failing to engage and utilize capable and trustworthy financial advisors (Figure 5). Even when they do engage a competent financial advisor, they sometimes fail to follow their advice. A more troubling reason, however, is that many professional athletes are subjected to financial fraud. It is a major problem! Fraud typically occurs when athletes blindly trust someone to care for their financial affairs and when they directly invest in a project without researching or understanding the risks of the transaction. That's what this book is about. You will be surprised by how often professional athletes are persuaded to invest their hard-earned money into transactions without safeguards, oversight and even without conducting a minimum amount of research before deciding to invest. It is like a recurring movie plot. The professional athlete is solicited to invest with promises of outsized returns. His investment is lost to a fraudulent scheme or outright theft. The con men, scam artists and fraudsters are eventually caught and usually brought to justice. Everyone else is surprised, shocked even, wondering how this continues to happen. In this book, I am going to tell you who does it, how it happens, why it happens, and what you can do to protect yourself from becoming the next victim.

FIGURE 5 – Why Professional Athletes Experience Financial Difficulties

1. Financial Fraud	**6. Domestic issues** -The professional athlete divorce rate is 60% - 80% -Childcare payments
2. Lack of competent financial planning	7. Medical issues
3. Failing to accept and follow sound financial advice	8. Legal problems
4. "Get rich quick" schemes and failing to seek legal, investment and tax advice from competent professionals	9. Failure to prepare for a career following athletics
5. Unreasonable financial support to family and friends	10. Unrealistic expectations about the length of careers

Financial professionals, agents, attorneys, teammates, and even family members defraud professional athletes. It may be hard to believe, but the stories included in this book are real and the losses incurred hurt professional athletes and their families. The National Football League Players Association (NFLPA) has taken a first step by creating a Registered Financial Advisors program. The program is intended to provide some level of protection for its athletes by screening individuals who seek to do business with the players. However, the NFLPA cannot and does not recommend any of those financial advisors. Instead, they run background checks and consider the history of applicants to ensure they meet minimum standards of criteria for ethical conduct in the financial services industry. However, it is important to note that just because a financial advisor is on the list does not mean they are beyond reproach and without flaws. In fact, some of the financial advisors highlighted in this book were approved for inclusion in the NFLPA's program. Yet, at some point along their journey, they made bad decisions that called into question their integrity and professionalism. They perpetrated frauds that cost their clients millions of dollars. Remember, it is not the job of the professional sports leagues or even its individual teams to protect the financial futures of the players. That responsibility rests solely with the athlete. It is his responsibility and his alone!

BEWARE: AFFINITY FRAUD

According to the SEC's Office of Investor Education and Advocacy, affinity fraud refers to "investment scams that prey upon members of certain groups, such as religious or ethnic communities, the elderly, or professional groups. Deceivers who promote affinity scams frequently are—or pretend to be—members of the group. They enlist respected leaders from within the group to spread the word about the scheme, by convincing people that a fraudulent investment is legitimate and worthwhile. Often, the leaders themselves become unwitting victims of the fraudster's scheme."

Further, the SEC asserts that "[a]ffinity fraud almost always involves either a fake investment or an investment where the fraudster lies about important details (such as the risk of loss, the track record of the investment, or the background of the promoter of the scheme)." "These scams exploit the trust and friendship that exist in groups of people who have something in common. Because of the tight-knit structure of many groups, it can be difficult for regulators or law enforcement to detect an affinity scam."

Affinity fraud is a huge problem and professional athletes are vulnerable targets because they are a relatively small community, a fraternity of sorts, which has access to capital or at least the perception thereof. In a 2012 article, The Economist referred to a study conducted by consulting firm Marquet International, that identified more than 300 sizeable Ponzi schemes with combined losses for investors of $23 billion. Marquet estimated that up to half of those were affinity-based. The Economist concluded that it is difficult, if not impossible, to derive a definitive number of investment fraud cases because it is tough to identify and track smaller frauds. Yet, the article noted that the Federal Bureau of Investigation was at that time probing over 1,000 cases of investment fraud and estimated that in all, affinity-fraud losses in America could be as much as $50 billion.

One of the more highly publicized affinity fraud actions in recent memory involving professional athletes was orchestrated by Triton Financial, LLC, an investment firm that co-sponsored the Heisman Trophy Trust. Triton solicited investments from former professional football players, explaining that the proceeds raised would be used to acquire an insurance firm. In exchange for their investment, some of the investors were led to believe they would yield upwards of 32% return on their investments. Over a five-year period, while primarily relying on its connection to and reputation of former athletes, Triton is believed to have raised more than $8.4 million from roughly 90 investors. Unfortunately, the proceeds were not used to acquire an insurance company. Instead, Triton's founder, , pocketed the money for his personal use.

The Triton fiasco and other examples of fraudulent misconduct discussed throughout this book are classic examples of affinity fraud. Yet, not all affinity fraud cases garner the same level of media coverage. They are sometimes much smaller in scale but no less impactful to the victims. For example, a recent affinity fraud case that did not receive a lot of media coverage involved an insurance broker who was sentenced to federal prison after scamming several NBA and NFL athletes between 2008 and 2012. In that case, the insurance broker collected roughly $140,000 in premiums from professional athletes and led them to believe he had purchased insurance policies on their behalf, providing coverage and protection up to $5 million. In reality, he had not purchased any policies or secured any coverage.

Following an investigation by the U.S. Attorney's Office, the FBI and the Florida Department of Financial Services, the broker pled guilty to 11 counts of felony wire fraud, was sentenced to 21 months in prison, and ordered to pay $144,229 in restitution.

THE CULPRITS AND
SCAM ARTISTS

Professional athletes and other high-income, high profile individuals rely on agents, financial advisors, attorneys and other professionals to guide them through their careers and responsibly invest their income. Family members, friends and teammates can also significantly influence how athletes spend their time and money. However, there are times when the very people employed to advise professional athletes betray their trust and confidence by making financially unsound decisions or worse, engaging in fraudulent or deceitful practices to pocket investment funds for themselves. Shamefully, family and friends have also been known to participate in unscrupulous conduct that could be described as nothing less than betrayal.

The purpose of this section is not to cast doubt or aspersion over an athlete's professional advisors, family members or friends, but to highlight risks they assume and provide several examples of when athletes were defrauded by someone in their circle of influence. In doing so, I intend to hammer home the notion that professional athletes should never blindly entrust their financial future to anyone. Instead, they should remain engaged, demand transparency and have a solid understanding of any contract they sign or investment they make.

AGENTS

There is no professional sports agent more famous than Jerry Maguire, the fictitious character played by Tom Cruise in the 1996 blockbuster movie. "Show me the money!" became a popular catchphrase, and summed up the responsibilities of sports agents to their professional athlete clients. More recently, shows such as HBO's *Ballers* glamorize the sports agent business and gives a glimpse, even if exaggerated, into the lives of professional athletes and the high-powered agents that represent them.

Like Jerry Maguire, real-life sports agents identify and pursue revenue-generating opportunities for their clients; however, their duties extend beyond merely "showing their clients the money." Sports agents negotiate player contracts, pursue endorsement deals, and manage a variety of complex marketing, legal and financial issues. Sometimes they even provide business, consulting and investment services. There is nothing inherently criminal or illegal about agents providing these ancillary services, but they should not be providing financial investment advice without the requisite training, certifications and credentials from the appropriate financial and regulatory authorities. Even if agents are qualified to provide investment services, I would adamantly caution any athlete against allowing his or her sports agent to be dual-hatted as their financial advisor. Why? Simply stated, business and investment services provide the greatest opportunity for agents to defraud their clients or mismanage their wealth.

Arguably the most infamous case of agent fraud in the history of professional sports involved then super-agent William H. Black, known throughout the sports world simply as "Tank." Tank was co-founder of Professional Management, Inc., an agency that represented a fairly high profile list of professional athletes in the National Football League (NFL) and the National Basketball Association (NBA). His client roster included some of the most recognizable names in sports, including running backs Fred Taylor and Duce Staley, wide receiver Sterling Sharp, and basketball phenom Vince Carter who had just begun setting the NBA ablaze with other worldly displays of dazzling dunks that not only rivaled those of Michael Jordan and Dominique

Wilkins in their primes, but raised the bar for dunk contest participants that would follow.

By all accounts, Tank was a talented and skilled contract negotiator, signing several first-round draft picks and closing lucrative player contracts for his high-profile clients. However, by his own admission, Tank got caught up in the lifestyle. He wanted more! Tank sought new ways to make more money and began offering business and consulting services through an affiliated firm, Professional Management Consulting, Inc. (PMI). It was through his PMI dealings that Tank admits he "got into lines that were gray or blurred….and [he] crossed them." Federal authorities and the Securities and Exchange Commission (SEC) accused Tank of mismanaging his clients' money and defrauding nearly two-dozen athletes of roughly $15 million that they had entrusted him to invest on their behalf. Following a trial, the United States District Court in the Northern District of Florida sentenced Tank to serve 60 months in prison and ordered him to pay $12 million in restitution.

Among Tank's alleged victims was Jacksonville Jaquar's running back standout, Fred Taylor. "Freddy T," as he is known to many of his friends, lost a reported $3.6 million in Tank's purported scams. Freddy T shared a special bond with Tank and saw him somewhat as a father figure. In Freddy's eyes, Tank could do no wrong and initially defended him when news of the alleged fraud became public. But as truth reared its ugly head, reality took its toll on Freddy's outlook and his relationship with Tank. At trial, Freddy testified against Tank, stating he "trusted that Tank would do right with the money." Unfortunately, that does not appear to have been the case. Following the alleged fraud, Freddy struggled financially for a period of time and certainly endured undue emotional stress. However, unlike many professional athletes who are the victims of fraud, Freddy T rebounded and, thanks to a lengthy career, recovered financially. In fact, reports indicate that Freddy T has since forgiven Tank and even calls the situation a blessing in disguise. Rightfully so—he now teaches his children about investing and his story is one that should no doubt resonate with other professional athletes on their journey.

Real Talk: Tank also pled guilty to allegations of money laundering, mail and wire fraud, and obstruction of justice for his alleged involvement with a drug dealer and was separately charged for illegally recruiting college players. But, to this day, Tank denies that he ever participated in any fraud relating to his professional athlete clients. It is not my intent to judge, or argue that he did or did not. Rather, my purpose is to educate professional athletes of the risk they assume when an agent also provides business consulting, financial advisory or investment services to them. Among other allegations against Tank, he was accused of making materially false and misleading statements and omissions to induce his clients to invest and failed to disclose to them the commissions and other fees he pocketed in the process.

The Lesson: The lesson here is simple: recognize that there are inherent conflicts of interest and you will expose yourself and your financial future to unnecessary risk when your agent also manages your money or tells you where and how to invest it.

FINANCIAL ADVISORS

Successful investment advisors combine analytical ability, comprehensive fiscal knowledge and superb customer service skills to help clients define and reach their financial goals. Because financial advisors are entrusted as fiduciaries, they are held to strict standards when it comes to their duties and responsibilities. In fact, fiduciaries are legally required to put the needs of their clients before their own, avoid conflicts of interest and operate with full transparency. Among the duties an investment advisor performs is discussing financial goals and educating clients on various ways to accomplish them. This includes providing an overview of investment alternatives and explaining how each can benefit, or hinder, the client's objectives.

Investment advisors help clients assess how aggressive they can be with their investments and the amount of risk they are willing to bear. In investing jargon, this is known as an investor's *risk tolerance*. In making that assessment, the advisor must consider the client's long- and short-term goals, family status, age, employment and expenses to give the most accurate advice. Once investment advisors establish the client's goals, needs and risk tolerance, they must research and analyze investments, strategies and market conditions to determine which options are most appropriate given the individual investor's unique circumstances. Even after an investment is made, the best advisors will continue to remain abreast of market trends and financial news to ensure their guidance continues to be accurate and relevant.

After conducting the required research, investment advisors put forward an investment strategy designed to help the client achieve his or her goals. The plan should include alternatives for investing in more than one type of asset, such as investing in stocks and bonds to diversify the client's portfolio and mitigate risk. Also, when the client experiences a life change, such as marriage, the birth of a child, a new job or retirement, investment advisors should reassess the investment strategy to determine if the current approach remains sound and recommend changes if necessary. In the absence of major events, advisors should still monitor and review client portfolios with regularity and propose adjustments and modifications whenever necessary to ensure the integrity of client accounts.

Because investment advisors work with sensitive financial information, they have a responsibility to keep detailed records of the services they provide. These include signed contracts, disclosure statements, advisory reports and other client documents, as well as clear documentation of invoices, payments received and the exact services rendered. The need for rigorous record keeping is magnified by the possibility of government agencies such as the SEC or Internal Revenue Service (IRS) requesting documentation or conducting an audit on the advisor or the client.

In addition, investment advisors are required to possess thorough knowledge of federal and state laws regarding investments and must adhere to the regulations and requirements of the SEC, the Financial Industry Regulatory Authority (FINRA) and any certifying bodies, such as the Certified Financial Planner Board of Standards, where necessary.

As stated earlier, federal law requires that investment advisors abide by stringent ethics rules to ensure impartial, good faith advice. This is sometimes referred to as a "fiduciary duty," and requires that investment advisors place the financial well-being of the client above their own. In addition, they are required to disclose all relevant information about an investment, avoid conflicts of interest, and acknowledge any payment or other compensation they receive for recommending certain products or investments.

Unfortunately, some investment advisors fail to honor their ethical obligations and fall short of their fiduciary duties. In search of riches, some even operate their business with blatant disregard of laws, regulations and guidance required by state and federal authorities. Jeff Rubin, a former financial advisor to many professional athletes, provides a stunning case study of how an otherwise seemingly legitimate financial advisor ended up on the wrong side of the law and allegedly defrauded many of his professional athlete clients out of millions of dollars.

Ironically, Jeff Rubin gained notoriety and the trust of many professional athletes when he was credited with exposing Tank Black's alleged fraudulent and deceitful activity. According to public records, Jeff was a properly credentialed investment advisor, registered in the States of Florida and Texas. He held the necessary licenses and certifications required by FINRA and was employed by two broker-dealers registered with the SEC. He was even registered in the NFLPA's financial advisor program, which by its own account was created to provide players with an additional layer of protection - not just from poor financial advice, but also from outright fraud. With these credentials, it would seem that Jeff was just the kind of person to trust with your finances.

In addition to working as an investment advisor, Jeff founded Pro Sports Financial, Inc. in 2007 to provide professional athletes concierge services such as paying monthly bills, procuring life insurance policies, booking travel, handling tax returns, and setting up trusts for family members. With his investment advisory business and concierge service offering, Jeff boasted a star-studded client roster that included an estimated 100 professional athletes, including Jevon Kearse, Santana Moss, Ray Lewis, Clinton Portis, Plaxico Burress, Fred Taylor, Frank Gore, Terrell Owens and others. According to reports, he even did business with boxing legend Floyd "Money" Mayweather. Sadly, Jeff allegedly convinced many of those athletes to invest in a series of speculative real estate transactions, including a failed casino project, without explaining the nature of the risks involved and without having a reasonable basis for believing the transactions were suitable for each client given their unique personal financial situations. In total, the failed casino project alone cost roughly 30 NFL players nearly $60 million in losses.

Even more insulting is that federal regulators claimed that Jeff actually pocketed $600,000 of the money he raised from his clients in connection with the failed casino investment and used the money to fund his lavish lifestyle. His failure to disclose the sums he pocketed was a direct violation of federal securities laws. In addition, Jeff was accused of opening illegitimate bank accounts, making extraordinary withdrawals from player's accounts without their authorization and diverting player's bank statements in order to hide the activity in their accounts. Once discovered, Jeff became the subject of several civil lawsuits, fined $250,000 and barred from many aspects of the financial services industry, including managing client money.

Real Talk: According to reports, Jeff also received a significant discount on the purchase price of his home in an upscale community in Florida by convincing NFL players to buy their homes from the developer. It does not appear that Jeff ever disclosed this fact or his underlying motivation to his clients. Even worse, forensic price analysis shows that property values on the players' homes declined as much as 60% following their purchases. In the end, several players lost their homes in foreclosure actions or were forced to sell at significant losses. The developer eventually pled guilty to bribery, money laundering, and other charges and was sentenced to 80-months in prison. It was later determined that the luxury home builder, Jeff's friend, had twice filed for bankruptcy and was convicted six times on fraud and other economic crimes.

According to FINRA, Jeff's case demonstrates how broker and investment advisor misconduct targets high-income, inexperienced and vulnerable investors. Like Tank, Jeff took advantage of professional athletes who placed their trust in him. And, while Jeff may well have engaged in unethical behavior, it did not absolve the athletes of their responsibility to enact safeguards to protect themselves and their assets.

Had a reasonable amount of due diligence been conducted, several red flags would have cautioned many of the athletes from entrusting Jeff. For example, Y! Sports reported that in 2003 NFL linebacker Barrett Green found discrepancies with Jeff's handling of his money. In 2004, Jeff settled a complaint with financial regulators pertaining to a complaint filed by NFL linebacker Johnny Rutledge, who claimed that several insurance documents were forged. The alleged forgeries costs Rutledge $119,000. In addition, Buffalo Bills wide receiver, Roscoe Parrish, won a judgment against Rubin because he allegedly formed companies in Parish's name without his consent.

The Lesson: Conduct thorough due diligence before entrusting an investment advisor with your money. If the investment advisor introduces you to investment opportunities, you should conduct due diligence on those companies and the principal players operating those businesses. Enact safeguards to protect your assets and get a second set of eyes to independently verify that the investment advisor and the investment opportunities are legitimate. It may cost you a small amount upfront but it can save you millions in the long run.

LAWYERS

The role of your attorney is to be your legal advocate, that is, to provide you with competent and timely legal representation and act in your best interest to help you resolve legal issues and avoid legal problems. An individual's relationship with his or her attorney should be one based on trust and confidence. Unfortunately, some attorneys and their law firms violate the solemn oath they take to perform their duties faithfully, impartially, and in the best interest of their clients. A Chicago-based tax attorney, Gary Stern, appears to have done just that when he allegedly created and oversaw an abusive tax-shelter scheme and facilitated sham transactions while working at the otherwise reputable Midwestern based law firm of Chuhak & Tecson. According to its website, the firm's history dates back nearly 30 years and is home to some 66 attorneys and more than 70 professional and support staff. By all accounts, Chuhak & Tecson appears to pride itself on its Midwestern values and maintains a solid standing within the community it serves. Yet, one of its own engaged in unethical practices that called into question an otherwise reputable law firm.

In general, tax shelters are not necessarily illegal and in many instances are explicitly authorized under federal and/or state tax laws. Without getting too granular, a tax shelter can provide significant benefits as it offers taxpayers who make qualified investments the ability to reduce their state and federal tax liabilities. The key, however, is that any tax shelter must be structured properly to comply with prevailing tax laws and policies of the Internal Revenue Service (IRS). Otherwise, the IRS and/or state tax authorities can disqualify the so-called tax shelter and subsequently pursue taxpayers for tax payments, interest and penalties. Unfortunately, that is exactly what happened to as many as 20 NFL players who invested in the so-called tax shelters allegedly created by Stern and promoted by Chuhak & Tecson. Among those who suffered losses and filed lawsuits against Stern and the firm were quarterback Kyle Orton, wide receiver Terrell Owens, and Hall of Fame linebacker, Ray Lewis.

In the lawsuits, the plaintiffs alleged misrepresentation, negligence, breach of fiduciary duty and fraud and sought $10 million in damages. Specifically, they argued that Stern and his partners never disclosed that there was a possibility that the investors would not receive tax credits because the tax shelter entities did not meet regulatory requirements. In fact, several players stated that they invested in the so-called tax shelters only after receiving assurances from Stern that the regulatory requirements had been satisfied.

Following an audit, the IRS disqualified more than 90% of tax the credits promoted by Stern. Surprisingly, there was evidence suggesting that Stern intentionally set up companies and partnerships to facilitate sham transactions in an attempt to qualify for tax shelters. Making matters worse, Stern allegedly transferred the tax credits after shunning the advice of a colleague in his office who wrote a memo explaining that the tax credits could not be legally transferred and therefore would not provide the benefits for which they were being structured. When Stern received a copy of the memo, he allegedly revised it to falsely assure his clients that the transactions were legal.

When the investigation and legal proceedings concluded, authorities determined that Stern had helped hundreds of clients falsely claim more than $16 million in improper tax credits. According to the Department of Justice, Stern and his business associates profited handsomely, keeping most of the money contributed to the scheme.

In the end, Stern was permanently barred from promoting tax fraud schemes and from preparing related tax returns.

Real Talk: As an investor, I am always amazed at how people will so blindly follow others on the hope that they will somehow make fortunes, or as in this case, evade taxes. In the world of investing, this is what we call the "herd mentality." Blindly investing with the herd is not only illogical, it can be detrimental to your financial health. Think about it. Why would you blindly make the same investments as everyone else when your financial situation, risk tolerance, age, family circumstances, and investing prowess are likely unique and therefore different from others in the herd? At the very least, you should consider your personal circumstances and conduct the research necessary to determine whether a particular investment is right for you and your family. Do not make decisions to invest blindly, simply based on the fact that your teammates or colleagues are making the same investment. A word of caution: When the herd gets slaughtered, so will you!

As an attorney, I am also baffled when I read or hear stories of an individual attorney representing a group of people making a substantial investment in a transaction. This, to me, is nothing more than another variation of the herd mentality. It is not possible for that attorney to know and take into account the individual needs and preferences of each potential investor in a large group. Certainly there are times when it makes sense to have a "lead attorney" or for one attorney to represent a group (e.g., class action lawsuits), but in most other instances there will be unavoidable conflicts of interest. For example, when the IRS initiated its investigation, Stern and his colleagues at Chuhak & Tecson represented all of the investors that were involved in the tax shelter transactions. However, as the firm and its partners became entangled in the investigation and subsequent legal proceedings, it abandoned the investors and abruptly withdrew its representation, claiming the firm was caught in a conflict of interest in its representation of both sides of the deal. The firm did the right thing by withdrawing but the damage was already done.

> ***The Lesson:*** When it becomes clear that one attorney or law firm is representing a large group in connection with an investment, I urge individual investors to engage their own legal counsel to provide an independent review and analysis of the deal. Of course, it may be impractical for each investor and attorney to have a seat at the table, but your personal attorney should be able to provide an objective perspective of the transaction and educate you on its risks and potential rewards before you make the investment.

BUSINESS PARTNERS

A business partnership can easily be compared to marriage because those that are successful typically share a common set of core values. Importantly, both require commitment, mutual trust and respect. Both are also impacted, positively or negatively, by decisions about money, its availability and whether to spend, save or invest. In short, both require a conscious choice, each and every day, to continue working towards a common goal with someone other than yourself. And that is not always easy!

Marriages and business partnerships fail for a variety of reasons, but many times a separation or divorce is easily linked to a violation of trust where at least one of the parties is unwilling or unable to honor the relationship's core values. In our society, it is a commonly held belief that maintaining a happy and healthy marriage over an extended period of time is almost impossible. However, the truth is that a business partnership is far more difficult to maintain. Recent reports have shown that, whereas 50% of marriages end in divorce, approximately 80% of business partnerships fail. Unfortunately, Sergei Fedorov, a former star in the National Hockey League, experienced both in a relatively short period of time and lost millions in the process.

Fedorov was a hockey legend that seemingly had it all. He was among the first Russian hockey players to gain notoriety in the NHL and helped lead the Detroit Red Wings to three Stanley Cup championships. At that time, he was considered to be amongst the historical greats. He also dated and then married Anna Kournikova, a professional tennis player and model who was known just as much for her physical beauty as she was for her play on tour. By all accounts, Fedorov was "The Man!" Until he wasn't...

Early in his career, Fedorov signed a $38 million, six-year deal, then considered one of the most lucrative contracts in NHL history. Around that same time, he met Joseph Zada through a mutual friend. Zada was a popular local business man and investor with ties to affluent suburbs of Detroit, Michigan and West Palm Beach, Florida. He flaunted the appearance of wealth, lived a lavish lifestyle and even had close ties to the chief executive officer of a Fortune 500 company. He partnered with and invested on behalf of athletes, doctors, veterinarians and even public service associations who starved for hefty returns on their investments. He promised profits of more than 20% in some cases and that is exactly what he delivered, so thought his investors.

After meeting Zada, Fedorov invested $150,000 with him. Like everyone else who had invested with Zada, Fedorov was more than pleased with the returns he received. Fedorov began to entrust Zada with more of his money and before long had invested more than $43 million with Zada. Just as he promised his other business partners and investors, Zada had persuaded them to believe he would make them rich (or richer, in Fedorov's case), primarily by using his connections with the royal family in Saudi Arabia to invest in oil. He told some investors that a late sheik was his lover, while he told others that he was the sheik's illegitimate son. He even hosted a party attended by a Saudi Arabian prince and princess to affirm his connections in the middle east. But it was all a lie. The "prince" and "princess" at the party were actually paid actors and Zada fabricated his connection to the royal family.

According to the SEC and to everyone's surprise, Zada did not make any investments in oil. Rather, he ran an illegitimate business enterprise and was charged criminally with 15 counts of fraud and three charges of making false statements on loan applications in order to steal at least $20 million from 20 investors over a nearly 12-year period. In addition, civil proceedings initiated by the SEC resulted in a $120 million judgment against Zada—$56 million he allegedly stole from investors in connection with a Ponzi scheme, $8.5 million in interest and another $56 million for not showing any remorse.

U.S. District Judge Kenneth Marra presided over Zada's criminal trial. Judge Marra stated that Zada was one of the most skilled con men he had ever encountered. At the conclusion of the trial, there was enough evidence to convict Zada and sentence him to more than 17 years in prison, which was the maximum he could receive under federal sentencing guidelines.

Real Talk: Fedorov's decision to partner with Zada and massively increase the size of his investments cost him dearly. While dealing with a bitter divorce from his then wife, Fedorov was also engaged in a lengthy and tenuous battle with Zada, someone he trusted as a business partner. Somehow the foundation of his marriage and business partnerships crumbled because one or more of the foundational core values that presumably underpinned those relationships had been compromised. I cannot speak to what happened with his marriage to Kournikova, but clearly his business partnership with Zada was undermined by Zada's greed and his lack of commitment, trust and respect.

In the end, Fedorov and Zada reached a settlement that would require Zada to repay upwards of $60 million to Fedorov. Only one problem! To date, Zada has been unable or unwilling to pay. In the meantime, Fedorov allegedly suffered through three bank foreclosures and a host of other financial problems.

The Lesson: Fedorov and many of Zada's other victims indicated that they saw how lavishly he lived and because of his lifestyle, they assumed he knew what he was doing. They even admitted investing with Zada with little or no documentation. To add insult to injury, Zada's defense attorney argued that the lack of paperwork was evidence that the investors were simply loaning money to Zada, not investing with him. Let this be an example: NEVER invest with anyone without adequate paperwork explicitly stating the intended purpose and use of your money, where it will be held and under what circumstances your money will be returned. Any business partnership or investment MUST be properly documented to reflect those matters that are most important to the relationship.

TEAMMATES

It is not uncommon or even surprising when we learn that a professional athlete may have been the victim of some sort of fraud or financial scam. What is rare, shocking even, is when a professional athlete is actually perpetrating the fraud or engaging in predatory practices designed to unjustly enrich himself at the expense of his teammates or other professional athletes. That appears to be precisely what happened when one of the NFL's very own, Will Allen, allegedly stole millions of dollars from other professional athletes who invested with him and a business associate. Following investigations by the U.S. Attorney's Office and the SEC, Allen was arrested, accused of operating a Ponzi scheme and charged criminally with committing 23 felonies, including wire fraud, conspiracy to commit wire fraud and aggravated identity theft.

By all measures, Allen had a respectable NFL career, playing more than 10 years primarily with the New York Giants and Miami Dolphins. He signed contracts totaling more than $30 million, which one would assume would have set him up for a comfortable retirement when his playing days were over. However, it became abundantly clear through the investigations that Allen was anything but comfortable. In fact, it appears that he was financially distressed and had to call upon a former teammate to pay $20,000 to bail him out of jail. Unfortunately, as I stated in an earlier chapter, Allen is not the first nor will he be the last professional athlete to mismanage his or her finances and experience dire financial stress during or following their career. Ironically, it is that very fact that provided the opportunity for Allen to execute his scheme and take advantage of unsuspecting colleagues.

Professional sports contracts are typically structured so that players receive most, if not all, of their compensation during the course of the season. Knowing this, Allen was acutely aware that other professional athletes, like him, experienced cash flow shortfalls from time to time, particularly during the off-season. Identifying the opportunity, Allen and his business partner launched a business to make high-interest, short-term loans targeting those professional athletes who needed money while they waited to get paid from their sports contracts. To fund the "loans," Allen and his team raised about $31 million from 40 investors but misrepresented to them that the loans to athletes would be directly backed, or secured, by the athlete's contract. Furthermore, they falsely claimed that loan repayments could be received directly from the team with whom the athlete was currently assigned. Simply put, these representations were not true.

According to court filings, Allen allegedly made only one legitimate loan. The loan was made to a professional hockey player but Allen inflated its actual value, telling his investors that the loan would be for $5.65 million when in fact it was only $3.4 million. Allen is believed to have pocketed the difference. In addition, he is believed to have orchestrated five phantom, or fictitious, loans to three professional football players and two professional baseball players. In reality, no such loans were made and he allegedly forged signatures to make the transactions appear real.

Authorities argued that Allen and his associates knowingly or recklessly induced investors to participate in loans that were never made. Instead, bank records provide evidence that money obtained from investors was used to meet monthly payment obligations to other investors, to fund unrelated personal business ventures, and for Allen's personal expenses at "casinos, pawn shops, jewelers, grocery stores, cigar shops and clothing retailers…storage facilities, airlines, hotels, restaurants, night clubs, and limousine companies." In all, the SEC's complaint stated that Allen misappropriated $7 million, including $3.4 million in wire transfers to his personal bank account, $200,000 to a mortgage company to satisfy creditors judgments against him, credit card payments and expenses owed to a casino resort. Meanwhile, his business partner received over $200,000.

Real Talk: Ask anyone who has ever had a career in the NFL, NBA, MLB, NHL or any other professional sports league and you will find that they view it as a fraternity of sorts, a band of brothers. They share something in common that only a small fraction of the broader society can claim: they are among the most elite athletes on the planet and are the very best at their respective sport. It is a badge of honor. So, it comes as a surprise when someone like Will Allen, a longstanding member of the fraternity, selfishly betrays its trust and confidence for unjust and personal enrichment at the expense of his brethren. It's just not supposed to be this way! Yet, sometimes it is!

The Lesson: Yes, Allen was a member of the fraternity, but a basic amount of research should have been conducted before the 41 investors entrusted him with $31 million. At the very least, someone should have stopped and asked if Allen was qualified to operate the type of business he was pitching. They quickly would have determined that he did not have the requisite experience. And, even if they wanted to give him the benefit of the doubt, a basic level of due diligence would likely have revealed that Allen himself had multiple run-ins with the law, was under financial duress and had himself recently endured a bout with a predatory lender.

In a twist of irony, court records show that Allen received a $505,000 loan from Pro Player Funding, LLC in October 2010. Incredibly, he was allegedly charged an interest rate of 34% per year. Allen failed to fulfill his obligations under the agreement and, within two months, defaulted on the loan. Pro Player Funding sued Allen and, in March 2011, won a default judgment in excess of $576,000. If not a red flag, this type of information should certainly raise a yellow flag for any investor!

FAMILY AND FRIENDS

When your agent, financial advisor, attorney, business partners and teammates fail you, you can always depend on your family, right? No doubt, we would all like to think that. Unfortunately, there is enough evidence to suggest that it may not be the wisest decision for professional athletes to mix their business and family affairs. While there are certainly success stories of families working together to build wealth that transcends generations and secures the family's financial future, there are far too many tales of families being torn apart and wealth being destroyed because of greed, unrealistic expectations of entitlement and inadequate oversight. Just ask professional baseball player Ryan Howard, who recently endured a very public battle with his family over his personal finances.

Ryan was a gifted athlete, taking Major League Baseball by storm in 2005 when he was named National League Rookie of the Year. In 2006, he was named National League Most Valuable Player and would go on to become a multi-year All-Star playing first base for the Philadelphia Phillies. By 2014, Ryan had earned $130 million playing the game he loved.

By all accounts, Ryan was a dedicated family man and shared a close bond with his parents, identical twin brother Corey, and his other two siblings. Ryan was earning a fortune, and like many other professional athletes, wanted his family to benefit from his success. He allegedly purchased a BMW for his mother, an Aston Martin for his father, and Mercedes Benz trucks for both of his brothers. But Ryan did not stop there. He wanted to ensure that his family would never again experience financial hardship, so he established a company called RJH Enterprises, into which he invested $8 million, to market his future earnings potential and effectively serve as a quasi-trust fund for his family. RJH Enterprises employed everyone in the Howard clan, including his father as business manager, mother as chief financial officer, one brother as general counsel, the other (his twin brother) as co-manager and director of marketing and personal support services, and his sister as executive director of the Ryan Howard Family Foundation.

Based on court records, RJH Enterprises paid the family members nearly $3 million. So, what was the problem? Ryan was not aware of the extent of the payments and disbursements being made to family members until he made the decision to get more involved and assume personal responsibility over his financial affairs. Court records show that Ryan's father alone was paid over $1.3 million. Ironically, when Ryan reached the professional ranks of baseball, his father Ron adamantly cautioned him against working with third-party professionals to manage his personal and financial affairs. He warned that managers, consultants, advisors and other third-party professionals could "rob him blind and leave him financially unprepared for life after baseball." Ron urged that the way to avoid those problems was to put "his business, personal and financial affairs in the hands of family members, who had 'valuable skills' and whom Ryan could trust." To Ryan, it sounded reasonable… and coming from his father, it seemingly made sense. A major flaw in Ron's plan, however, was that none of the Howard's are believed to have had any background or experience with professional sports or handling the business affairs of professional athletes.

In 2012, Ryan assumed personal responsibility for RJH Enterprises and learned of the unauthorized payments. He confronted his parents and siblings and expressed concern that they were not protecting his interests but rather enriching themselves at his expense. According to court records, Ryan's father demanded as much as $10 million for them to walk away and refused to hand over the books and records of RJH Enterprises to Ryan. At that point, everything began to sour for the once close-knit family. Ryan sought to terminate the services of his family members and the claims and counterclaims began to fly. Even Ryan's twin-brother, Corey, filed suit against Ryan claiming $2 million in damages, arguing that Ryan unjustly terminated his contract. Ryan counterclaimed, arguing that Corey never performed any significant services even though he had been paid over $600,000. Furthermore, according to Ryan's counterclaim, Corey engaged in a conspiracy with their father, mother and brother to defraud RJH Enterprises and that his actions were willful, wanton and malicious. The lawsuits were eventually settled for undisclosed amounts but several years of expensive legal maneuvering, frustration, and embarrassment clearly took a toll on Ryan, a once close-knit family and a promising career. Sadly, it appears that the Howard family bond is forever fractured and it is highly doubtful that their once close relationship will ever be the same.

Real Talk: Like me, many professional athletes were not born and raised in the wealthiest homes and communities. Once we have made a few dollars, one of the first things we want to do is "take care" of everyone in the family. That is admirable, but not always the smartest thing to do early in your career, before you have set a solid foundation. Plus, nothing will rip a family apart quicker than finances. If you entrust your wealth and business affairs to family members who lack relevant experience, subject matter expertise, and objectivity, you are destined to witness your fortune crumble and you too will find yourself at odds with your relatives.

One article surmised that Ryan Howard's financial success might have cost him his family. I disagree. Ryan's success was not the problem. Ryan's decision to enlist his family to manage his financial affairs is what cost him. According to reports, Ryan's family members were not qualified to do the job he enlisted them to do. Interestingly, it was later revealed that some potential sponsors and business partners chose not to do business with Ryan and RJH Enterprises because his family members were incredibly difficult to deal with. So, not only did his family allegedly take money from him, they also kept him from receiving potentially lucrative sponsorships, endorsements and other business deals.

A more prudent approach, one that I strongly recommend is that professional athletes build a team of third-party professionals to manage their affairs. Do not place the power to control all of your financial affairs in the hands of any one person, even a trusted family member. If you want to gainfully engage or employ family members, consider having them provide independent oversight of fees being billed by, and payments being made to, third parties. A check and balance of sorts. Even then, ensure that they have or obtain the requisite training to do the job effectively. You can also create a reward system and incentivize them for identifying overbillings, overpayments and discrepancies. Ultimately, however, the professional athlete should maintain personal responsibility for his or her own affairs and maintain signature authority over all financial accounts.

The Lesson: My advice to any professional athlete in Ryan's position is DO NOT hire your family members to manage your financial affairs. If you do, you have set the foundation for family turmoil in the event that they achieve sub-par results, engage in unethical behavior, demand higher payouts or you decide for whatever reason to terminate their services.

Critically, you should never sign any document unless you read and understand what it means. In Ryan Howard's case, he allegedly signed several documents presented to him by family members without reviewing them and was never given copies of the agreements. Never fall into that trap! Always know WHAT you are signing and WHY you are signing it!

THE SCHEMES

UNAUTHORIZED INVESTMENTS

An investment is unauthorized if it is made without the investor's consent and approval. A textbook example of an unauthorized investment was orchestrated by Blazer Capital Management and its founder, Martin Blazer III. In 2008, Blazer founded his firm to provide what he described as premium personal advisory services to professional athletes, entertainers, and high net worth individuals and their families. Specifically, he offered investment advisory services, bill pay services, personal budgeting and tax payment services. By April 2013, Blazer had 21 clients and managed over $15 million in assets on a discretionary basis[1], which effectively allowed him to effect certain transactions from client accounts without having to seek their approval for each and every transaction. Importantly, however, even in discretionary accounts, all decisions must be made in accordance with the client's stated objectives and goals and the client always retains the right to revoke such authority at any time.

At some point in 2009, Blazer agreed to raise approximately $1 million to fund two movie projects, in which he held a personal financial interest. Blazer solicited potential investors for the projects but was unsuccessful in raising the amount of capital he desired. After falling short of his goal, he approached one of his clients to invest in the project but the client refused, explicitly stating that he had no interest in the investment opportunity. Despite the client's explicit refusal, Blazer allegedly withdrew and transferred $500,000 from the client's account anyway to fund the movie projects. According to the ensuing SEC investigation, Blazer allegedly copied the client's signatures to

---

1 Discretionary accounts are distinguishable from non-discretionary accounts wherein clients make all transaction decisions and the financial professional simply reviews and executes it on behalf of the client.

create documents giving the appearance that the client had given him the authority to make the transfer.

When the client learned that Blazer had taken money from his account to invest in the movie projects without his authorization, the client threatened to sue Blazer and demanded that his money be returned. Unable to pay, Blazer then took $600,000 from another client's account to repay the first client and to make another unauthorized investment in a music venture. None of the transactions were approved and Blazer allegedly forged signatures to effect transfers from the accounts. Between 2010-2013, the SEC claimed that Blazer took $2.35 million from five clients, none of whom had approved transfers from their accounts, the investments in the movie projects or the investment in the music venture.

During the SEC's examination and subsequent investigation, Blazer falsely asserted that the transfers were authorized and even manufactured a series of documents to mislead the SEC staff into believing that the transactions were legitimate. In the end, Blazer agreed to settle the charges. However, as we have seen in other incidences of fraud, if his clients had conducted additional due diligence before dealing with Blazer, they would have learned that this was not the first time he faced allegations of defrauding athletes. With a quick Google search, they would have quickly surmised that Blazer had previous legal disputes with professional athletes over unpaid loans and in 2011, was sued for $4 million by a former NFL running back who accused him of misappropriating funds. That case too was settled out of court but the accusations of fraud and misappropriation should have cautioned investors to take a closer look into Blazer's record.

UNSUITABLE INVESTMENTS

An investment is deemed unsuitable when it is made on behalf of an investor but is not consistent with that investor's financial objectives and risk tolerance. It is the financial professional's job to ensure that any investment they recommend is suitable for their client. To be fair, no investment (other than outright scams) are inherently suitable or unsuitable; suitability depends on the investor's unique and individual circumstances. For example, for an elderly widow with limited financial resources and living on a fixed income, speculative investments such as options, futures and highly volatile penny stocks would be considered extremely unsuitable because the widow likely has a low risk tolerance. On the other hand, a young business executive with significant net worth and investing experience might be comfortable making those speculative investments as part of a diversified portfolio. In either case, an investment should be made in accordance with the objectives and risk tolerance of the individual investor, based on his or her age, income, assets and financial needs. Otherwise, an investment will likely be deemed unsuitable and therefore in violation of securities laws.

An SEC action against Billy Crafton and his firm, Martin Kelly Capital Management, provides a noteworthy case study on unsuitable investments. Crafton founded Martin Kelly Capital in 2006 with the expressed purpose of providing investment advice and wealth administration services to current and former professional athletes. By 2010, Crafton had built a solid business that included an impressive roster of well-known athletes. His business became so successful that Atlanta-based SunTrust Bank acquired his business for $2.7 million and named him head of its San Diego office to strengthen its Sports & Entertainment Specialty Group, which targeted professional athletes as its core client base. But, within six months, SunTrust Bank fired Crafton and he became the subject of the NFLPA's first-ever warning to certified athlete agents, informing them of an ongoing investigation by law enforcement authorities and providing a cautionary tale of an investment advisor who was investing his client's money in ill-advised and unsuitable ventures.

The SEC's investigation revealed that Crafton represented to his clients that he would employ a very conservative, safe and liquid investment strategy aimed at growth with little to no risk. Based on his clients' investment objectives, it was a prudent strategy and made perfect sense given that professional athlete careers are often short-lived and, in certain instances such as in the NFL, their income may not be guaranteed. Unfortunately, Crafton lied to his clients and, according to the SEC, he actually invested their money in high-risk, alternative investments that were "run, managed, controlled, operated and/or created by individuals with whom Crafton had a personal relationship, business dealings or kick-back agreements." The SEC charged that Crafton invested as much as 60% of his clients' assets into unsuitable, high-risk, privately held, unsecured and illiquid securities and he failed to disclose to his clients the conflicts of interest stemming from his personal financial interest in and close ties to each investment.

In one case, Crafton invested a substantial amount of his clients' assets into Westmoore Lending Opportunity Fund and other related entities but failed to disclose to his clients that he had received more than $1.5 million in payments for investing his clients' money in those funds. In addition, he allegedly received but failed to disclose another $466,000 in brokerage fees and direct payments. Even worse, the SEC declared that Westmoore was nothing more than a Ponzi-like scheme and a corporate shell game designed to defraud investors of more than $50 million. When his former employer, SunTrust Bank, warned the clients about the ongoing SEC investigation, Crafton allegedly launched a telephone and email campaign to assure the athletes that there was nothing wrong with their investments, that their money was safe and SunTrust Bank was simply trying to create problems and misstate facts to poach his clients. But it was too late. By that point, Crafton had been exposed and he failed in his attempt to conceal the fact that investments in the Westmoore entities were essentially worthless. The SEC concluded its investigation and charged him with fraudulent misconduct and violating federal securities laws. Crafton knew it was over! He agreed to settle with the SEC and separately pled guilty to criminal charges of conspiracy to commit wire fraud.

MISREPRESENTATION

Under State and federal securities laws stockbrokers, investment professionals and their firms are required to provide complete and factually accurate information about investments they recommend to their clients. Failing to do so or otherwise presenting information in a manner that is false or misleading can be the basis for a securities claim. Rightfully so! In simple terms, a financial professional that misrepresents material facts to clients regarding the sale or recommendation of an investment breaches a foundational duty of good faith owed to his clients. Similarly, an omission of material facts can be just as harmful. The bottom line is that investors deserve, and quite frankly should demand, timely, relevant and accurate information about the potential risks of an investment so that they can make informed decisions about whether to invest.

Sometimes an act of misrepresentation may not necessarily be intentional, yet the misstatements or omissions of material facts can result in significant financial losses and undermine the trust an investor has in the financial professional. For example, Horace Grant, who played in the NBA for a number of years with the Chicago Bulls and Los Angeles Lakers, sought and won an action against Morgan Keegan in 2009 after he suffered losses in connection with investments he made in mortgage-based bond funds. Grant argued that Morgan Keegan failed to fully disclose the nature of the risks involved by investing in such funds. It is reasonable to assume that Morgan Keegan did not intentionally mislead Grant and other investors in those bond funds but the firm violated its duty to educate investors and fully disclose the risks involved so the investors could make informed decisions. A FINRA arbitration panel agreed with Grant and ordered Morgan Keegan to pay at least $1.59 million to Grant.

At other times, material misstatements or omissions are perceived to be calculated and intentional and are perceived by regulators as outright fraud. FINRA's action against Success Trade Securities and its CEO and president, Fuad Ahmed, illustrates the point. Ahmed founded the Company in 1998 with the vision of building a discount online trading business intended to compete against the likes of popular online brokerage firms and trading platforms such as E*Trade. Investing heavily in the trading technology and having some early success, Ahmed wanted to expand his business but knew he would need additional capital. He set a target to raise $5 million, prepared a prospectus and promissory notes assuring returns to investors ranging from 12.5% to 26%. In the prospectus, Ahmed disclosed to his potential investors that the proceeds would be used for advertising, debt reduction, business expansion and the acquisition of an Australian broker dealer. Interest from potential investors was so profound that the company sold $19.4 million worth of the promissory notes, nearly four times the amount of Ahmed's initial target. According to FINRA, 65 investors purchased 152 promissory notes, investing amounts that ranged from as little as $6,500 to as much as $1 million. Of the total amount raised, approximately $12 million (or nearly 60%) came from young professional athletes in the NFL and NBA who, according to the SEC, were financially unsophisticated and did not qualify as accredited investors[2] as was required under securities laws. The professional athletes were introduced to the investment opportunity by a single broker, Jade Wealth Management, which had apparent conflicts of interest and questionable ties to Ahmed and his Company. Among the athletes believed to have purchased notes were Victor Cruz, Vernon Davis, Brandon Knight and others. No doubt the players likely had some level of comfort (albeit misguided) working with the broker because he was a registered financial advisor with the NFLPA.

According to FINRA, Ahmed and the Company misrepresented or omitted material facts which would have revealed to potential investors that the Company was actually in dire financial condition at the time of its offering. For example, the Company failed to disclose that it had suffered losses in almost every year of its existence and only had about half of the business it needed to break-even.

Moreover, the Company never amended its prospectus and other disclosures to alert the investing public that it was actually raising four times more than it initially sought and that it would use the proceeds in a manner not previously disclosed. While Ahmed's legal counsel

---

2 Under federal securities laws, a company may not offer or sell securities unless the transaction has been registered with the SEC or an exemption from registration is available. Once such exception allows for offers and sales of securities to so-called "accredited investors," which generally includes individuals who have earned income exceeding $200,000 (or $300,000 with a spouse) in each of the prior two years OR has a net worth over $1 million.

argued otherwise, FINRA claims that Ahmed used the proceeds from the offering to pay interest on notes issued to previous investors, in essence accusing him of running a Ponzi-scheme. In addition, Ahmed allegedly used some of the proceeds to cover personal expenses exceeding $800,000 for credit card bills, travel and a Range Rover lease payment of $1,300 per month. According to regulators, Ahmed even used proceeds from the offering to make nearly $100,000 in interest-free loans to his brother. None of these items appear to have been disclosed to investors.

In August 2015, regulators settled with Ahmed and the Company, ordering him to pay $27 million in restitution, interest, disgorgement and penalties. For its part in selling the promissory notes and failing to protect the interest of investors, FINRA barred Jade Wealth Management and its principal from the financial services industry. In addition, the NFLPA revoked its registration from the financial advisor program.

MISAPPROPRIATION

Misappropriation occurs when someone intentionally and illegally uses another person's money for one's own use and benefit rather than for or on behalf of the rightful owner. Ever since money was created, thieves have developed countless ways to steal money that does not belong to them. In some situations, the would-be thief is legitimately in possession of the money because the owner has entrusted him with it. If that person uses the money for his own purposes without the consent of the rightful owner, this is known as misappropriation, something that the victims of Kirk S. Wright now know all too well.

Wright, a native of Bronx, New York, was a well-educated African American male, someone who seemingly made his family and community proud. He overcame various challenges while growing up in the Bronx and attended Binghamton University, State University of New York before ultimately earning a master's degree in public administration from Harvard University.

After graduating from Harvard, Wright founded a group of seven investment funds branded under the "International Management Associates" moniker. By age 35, Wright had developed a stellar reputation for investing and had raised between $115 million and $185 million from more than 500 investors, including some of Atlanta's top African American doctors, entrepreneurs and business professionals, and at least six NFL players who collectively entrusted him with more than $20 million. Wright's investors were so impressed with him that they started to recruit their families, friends, colleagues and teammates to invest.

Unfortunately for those investors, Wright's acclaimed investing acumen wasn't just overstated, it was fabricated. In February 2006, the SEC filed a complaint and temporary restraining order against Wright and his firm to halt what it described as an ongoing fraud. According to the SEC's complaint, Wright was providing investors with quarterly statements that grossly misrepresented both the amount of assets he managed and the rates of return he generated.

The SEC concluded that Wright's misrepresentations were flagrant and that he blatantly provided false information to his investors. For example, according to the complaint, Wright sent statements to investors claiming that his funds had appreciated in excess of 20%. In reality, where Wright touted handsome returns, he had actually suffered substantial losses that were never disclosed to his investors.

In a separate incident, several investors demanded to see official brokerage account statements. Wright produced statements and even showed a website to one investor representative purporting to be from the broker-dealer that held his firm's accounts. The statements listed four separate accounts with combined assets exceeding $155 million. However, the SEC concluded in its investigation that three of the accounts did not exist and the fourth account did not belong to Wright or his firm. In short, Wright "fabricated and reflected assets which the fund did not possess at that time."

Wright not only lied to his investors, he falsified periodic forms that his firm was required to file with the SEC. In early 2006, his firm filed what is known as a Form ADV[3] in which it claimed that the firm managed approximately $185 million in assets. However, the SEC has concluded that the firm had less than $500,000 in its accounts and swiftly moved to initiate action against Wright. Authorities issued an arrest warrant for Wright, but he disappeared and went into hiding. He mysteriously made himself available for a telephone interview and when asked whether he used investor money to fund his lifestyle, Wright responded curtly: "I challenge you to find where I spent the money."

So, where did all the money go? To this day, only a fraction of the money has been accounted for. As one author noted, "[w]hat Wright didn't lose, he spent…" Wright owned six luxury vehicles - including a $200,000 Lamborghini, a $50,000 Rolex watch, completed a $1 million remodeling job on his mansion, and spent $500,000 on his wedding reception. Accounting for all of the money that disappeared has been impossible.

---

3 In general terms, Form ADV is a uniform form used by investment advisors to register with the SEC and state securities authorities. The document is publicly available and provides a wealth of information about the investment advisor's business, clients, practices, affiliates, compensation, fees, disciplinary actions, etc.

In the end, a jury deliberated for two days and Wright was convicted in federal court on 47 counts of mail fraud, securities fraud and money laundering. He was sentenced to 710 years in prison and ordered to pay $16 million in fines. Within days, however, Kirk Wright was found dead in his jail cell having committed suicide, while his investors were left searching for answers.

PONZI SCHEMES

Who can forget Bernie Madoff? He was the former non-executive chairman of the NASDAQ stock market who started his own investment firm and in 2008 shocked the world when he admitted that the firm he founded and ran for nearly 50 years was nothing more than a Ponzi scheme. While initial reports varied, the fraud was initially estimated to be in the range of $65 billion, easily making it the largest financial fraud in U.S. history.

Madoff's fraud may have been the largest Ponzi scheme ever uncovered, but it certainly was not the first. That credit generally goes to Charles Ponzi, the now infamous businessman and con artist whose name is forever linked to the scam. No doubt, throughout history there have been other examples of hustlers and criminals orchestrating similar schemes, but Ponzi's $20 million scam in 1919 provided the playbook for the Ponzi schemes we see today.

Ponzi, like Madoff, enticed new investors by offering investment returns that were abnormally high or unusually consistent. In executing his scheme, Ponzi promised investors a 50% profit within 45 days, or 100% profit within 90 days, by buying discounted postal reply coupons in other countries and redeeming them at face value in the United States as a form of arbitrage. In reality, Ponzi was paying early investors with the investments and proceeds he received from later investors, rather than from profits earned by the so-called arbitrage strategy.

Amazingly, nearly 100 years later and even after the heightened awareness that followed the Madoff scandal, the Ponzi scheme remains a favored tool of scam artist who bilk unsuspecting investors out of millions of dollars. Just ask NFL great and Hall of Famer, John Elway. He allegedly lost $15 million in a Ponzi scheme run by Sean Mueller and his company, Mueller Capital Management.

Mueller founded his firm in 2000, seemingly as a legitimate enterprise, employing what he described as a short-term day trading strategy that was designed to generate returns between 12% and 25%. He told investors that throughout the trading day he would hold up to 30 stock positions simultaneously but would minimize risk by holding no positions overnight. At its peak, regulators believed that Mueller had raised more than $120 million from 65 investors, including the money he raised from Elway and his business partner. As required, Mueller's firm provided monthly account statements to its investors. According to those statements, the firm never incurred a monthly loss and appeared to be generating handsome returns for its investors. However, an investigation in 2010 by the Colorado Division of Securities revealed a completely different reality. Investigators concluded that Mueller had provided to its investors, as well as its accountants, fictitious brokerage statements that led them to believe the firm was producing as he had promised. To the contrary, according to investigators, Mueller's firm suffered massive losses between 2008 and 2009. Those losses were never disclosed to investors and by April 2010 the firm actually had less than $9.5 million in cash and investments, but owed approximately $45 million to its investors.

Even worse, their analysis of the firm's bank records painted a picture that no one dared to imagine - Mueller was allegedly operating a Ponzi scheme and using proceeds he raised from new investors to help hide his losses. Adding insult to injury, Mueller is believed to have also used investor funds to live an extravagant lifestyle, purchasing luxurious homes, expensive cars, memberships in exclusive country clubs and to pay for daily personal living expenses. State regulators stepped in and closed Mueller's business and tried to recover as much money as possible to return to the investors. Unfortunately, regulators are believed to have recovered only around $10 million. Mueller ultimately pled guilty to his crimes and was sentenced to 40 years in prison for securities fraud, theft and racketeering charges.

Based on the findings of the investigation and subsequent legal proceedings, it appears that Mueller founded his company and initially operated it with good intentions. However, by his own admission, at the end of a quarter, the market went against him resulting in substantial losses. He panicked and sent out a falsified report. He then continued the scheme desperately trying to recover the money he had lost. The presiding judge in Mueller's case acknowledged that the case was not the typical fraud action motivated by greed and laced with bad intentions. Instead, Mueller's case was more ego and hubris. Still, to his investors, the result was all the same. They lost millions!

PUMP AND DUMP

A "pump and dump" is an illegal practice that occurs when a small group of people purchase shares of a company's stock, then overhype its prospects and potential before recommending it to other unsuspecting investors. The promoter who purchased the shares early and hyped its prospects, sells when he believes the price has peaked. The result is a quick spike in stock price followed by an equally fast downfall.[4] Most pump and dump schemes involve smaller publicly traded companies that are listed for trading on the over-the-counter bulletin board (OTCBB)[5]. They typically have low stock prices, a relatively small amount of its shares issued to the investing public and significantly less publicly available information upon which to conduct research. Furthermore, small company stock prices are generally much more volatile[6] than larger companies. Accordingly, small company stocks are more susceptible to manipulation.

I could easily write a separate book about the countless investors who have fallen victim to "pump and dump" schemes but one story worth sharing involves Daniel "Rudy" Ruettiger. You may recall Rudy from the popular movie whose title comes from his name and whose story is based on events of his life and his dream of wanting to play football for the Notre Dame Fighting Irish. Yes! That Rudy! The movie "Rudy" has been voted in some circles as one of the most inspiring movies of all time. "RUDY...RUDY...RUDY..." became the rallying cry for anyone who needs the motivation to push through obstacles or any team that sees itself as the underdog.

---

4 There is also a variation of this scam called the "short and distort." Instead of spreading positive news, fraudsters seek profits by executing a smear campaign to drive down the stock price. Profits are derived by implementing what is known as a short selling strategy.

5 The OTCBB is an electronic trading service that offers investors up-to-the-minute quotes, last-sale prices and volume information for certain equity securities. Unlike the Nasdaq and New York Stock Exchange (NYSE), there are minimal listing requirements for companies trading on the OTCBB.

6 Volatility refers to the amount of uncertainty or risk concerning the size of changes in a security's value. A higher volatility means that a security's value can potentially fluctuate over a larger range of values, meaning its price can change dramatically over a short time period in either direction. A lower volatility means that a security's value does not fluctuate dramatically, but changes in value at a steady pace over a period of time.

But, there is more to Rudy's story, events that transpired after the movie soared to popularity and "Rudy" became a beacon of hope for so many athletes who had dreams of their own. "Rudy" became a household name and he wanted to cash in on his popularity. In doing so, he partnered with a college friend to create Rudy Nutrition, a sports drink company intended to compete against Gatorade, PowerAde and others. His tagline: "Dream Big! Never Quit!" Believing he had an opportunity to capitalize on his popularity, Rudy and his partners converted Rudy Nutrition from a private company to a publicly traded company whose shares could trade on the OTCBB and be purchased and sold in the open market by individual investors.

In an effort to sell the shares of the company's stock to as many investors as possible, Rudy enlisted the services of a disbarred lawyer and an experienced penny stock promoter. A penny stock promoter is supposed to create buzz, hype and awareness around smaller publicly traded companies that do not have a wealth of publicly available information that potential investors can easily access. As discussed, if the promoter is successful, a company's trading volume and stock price could rise exponentially and the owners of the company and its early investors would profit handsomely if they sell their shares in a timely manner. The problem, however, is that stock promotion is a form of trading manipulation and fraud. Bottom line: it is illegal!

Rudy's stock promoters clearly did their job. They promoted the hell out of the company, making claims in press releases and promotional materials that Rudy's sports drink outperformed PowerAde in blind taste tests and outsold Gatorade in another test. On the hype, almost one billion shares of stock were sold to unsuspecting investors, and in just two weeks, the company's stock price skyrocketed from $0.25 to $1.05 per share, or 320%. A huge windfall for early investors!

However, according to the SEC, the promotional materials and press releases were not just hype, they were false, misleading and intended to deceive investors. The SEC concluded that it was a pump-and-dump scheme that generated more than $11 million in illegal profits. The Commission suspended trading of the company's shares and initiated legal action against Rudy and his partners, prohibiting them from participating in penny stocks and required them to repay their illicit profits and penalties. It was a sad ending to such an inspiring beginning.

PROTECTING YOURSELF
FROM FRAUD

THE BASICS

The threat of financial fraud and its potentially crippling impact on your financial security is very real. According to a study prepared for the Financial Industry Regulatory Authority Investor Education Foundation, 84% of Americans have been solicited with a potentially fraudulent investment offer. Given this stark reality, it is imperative to assume primary responsibility for protecting yourself against fraud. Do not delegate that task to anyone. However, build a team of credible professionals who will not only help you achieve your financial goals, but can collectively provide a system of checks and balances so that you do not become the victim of a fraudulent scheme.

At a minimum, I urge you to seek independent professional advice from neutral outside experts, such as an accountant, attorney or financial advisor who is not affiliated with the group promoting the investment. While it is not possible to rid the world of all fraud, the following guidance – some of which is recommended directly by the SEC, FINRA and other federal and state regulatory authorities – may prove useful in minimizing your risk of becoming a victim of fraud.

1. **Do not blindly trust what someone tells you about an investment opportunity, no matter the source.** Never make an investment based solely on the recommendation of another person. Conduct your own diligence and investigate the truthfulness of what you have been told because the person telling you about the investment may have good intentions, but may have been fooled themselves into believing that the investment is legitimate when, in reality, it is not.

2. **Beware of investments that promise unusually high profits or "guaranteed" returns.** If an investment seems too good to be true, it probably is. The SEC has repeatedly warned investors that promises of fast and high profits, with little or no risk, are classic warning signs of fraud. Very few investments are risk-free, so you should be cautious about claims to the contrary.

3. **Do not invest without a written agreement.** Handshakes and verbal promises are not enough. If there is no documentation or paperwork that formalizes the rights and obligations of all parties, do not make the investment. Written agreements and legal documentation not only sets forth the understanding of the parties, it also provides a basis upon which to initiate legal action if a party breaches the agreement in the future.

4. **Don't be pressured into making an investment and beware of the herd mentality.** Just because someone you know made money, or claims to have made money, on a previous or similar investment does not mean you will too. View with caution any investment promoted as a "once-in-a-lifetime" opportunity or claims to have "inside" or confidential information. Also, be cautious if the promoter employs high-pressure sales tactics or boasts that several members of a particular group are investing in the opportunity. Remember, if you follow the herd and the herd gets slaughtered, so will you!

5. **Avoid concentration.** Learn from the example of Curt Schilling. Never put all of our eggs in one basket. The former Boston Red Sox great lost more than $50 million on his video game company, 38 Studios. "I'm tapped out," he told a Boston radio station. "The money that I had earned and saved in baseball was all gone. ... I put everything in my name in this company." To minimize the risk of losing everything you have earned to a fraudulent scheme, diversify your investments and portfolio.

6. **Demand access to books and records.** Anytime you invest in a private transaction, you should negotiate for contractual rights to consult with management, receive financial statements, inspect and audit books and records, and any other provisions that you and your attorney believe will enable you to protect your investment.

7. **Maintain control over your financial affairs.** Never give any one person complete access to or control over your financial affairs. Beware of financial professionals who overemphasize the need for access to or control of your money. Only under limited circumstances should anyone be given discretionary investing or spending authority in your accounts. Even then, you must remain vigilant to protect your interests.

8. **Know Who You're Dealing With.** You have several tools at your fingertips to quickly check the backgrounds and disciplinary history of individuals and firms claiming to be financial professionals. Many of the tools are free of charge. For example, a quick search on Google can yield surprising results. In addition, you can review FINRA BrokerCheck reports at www.brokercheck.finra.org to access information about a broker's past customer complaints or disciplinary actions. For financial planners, the Certified Financial Planning Board maintains an excellent search tool at www.cfp.net that can be used to research whether a financial planner has had any disciplinary actions filed against them. Similarly, the SEC maintains a search tool for investment advisers at www.adviserinfo.sec.gov. However, like the NFLPA's registered financial advisor program, none of these tools provide a fail-safe mechanism against fraud or financial misconduct. Yet, each provides a mechanism to learn more about an individual or firm before you decide to do business with them and entrust them with your financial future.

9. **Review Your Account Statements.** At least monthly, you should review your account statements (bank, brokerage, credit card, etc.) to ensure that all transactions shown are ones that you actually made or authorized. If you see a mistake on your statement or do not receive a statement, immediately contact your financial institution.

10. **Report suspicious activity.** If you notice unauthorized activity on your account or believe you may be the victim of fraud, immediately contact your attorney. You should also report any suspicious activity or perceived wrongdoing to the SEC, FINRA or your state securities regulators. Contact details for each are provided below:

U.S. Securities and Exchange Commission (SEC)
Office of Investor Education and Advocacy
100 F Street, NE
Washington, DC 20549-0213
Telephone: (800) 732-0330
Fax: (202) 772-9295

Financial Industry Regulatory Authority (FINRA)
FINRA Complaints and Tips
9509 Key West Avenue
Rockville, MD 20850
Telephone: (301) 590-6500
Fax: (866) 397-3290

North American Securities Administrators Association (NASAA)
750 First Street NE
Suite 1140
Washington, DC 20002
Telephone: (202) 737-0900
Fax: (202) 783-3571

AVOID CONCENTRATION

In the investing world, investors are often encouraged to maintain a level of diversification in their portfolios. In general, "diversification" is the process of allocating capital in a variety of investments in order to reduce the risk of loss or exposure to any one particular asset. When an investor's portfolio lacks diversification, it is considered "concentrated" because the investor has typically only invested in a single or handful of investments. The fewer assets that an investor holds, he exposes himself to a greater risk of loss should an investment fail. That is exactly what happened to Sergei Fedorov when he invested and lost nearly all of his career earnings to con man Joseph Zada. Fedorov's story was the subject of an earlier chapter but he is by no means the only athlete or investor to suffer grave financial harm because he concentrated too much of his wealth in a single investment. Ask Curt Schilling! Even though he was not a victim of fraud, he knows all too well the effects of concentration when an investment fails. In laymen's terms, Schilling - like Fedorov - put all of his eggs in one basket. He tried to hit a home run...but struck out.

By the time he retired in 2009, Schilling was widely considered one of the most dominant pitchers of his era during his career in Major League Baseball. He is one of only 16 pitchers in the history of baseball to strikeout more than 3,000 batters. Schilling won countless awards, won the World Series three times and was named World Series Most Valuable Player in 2001. Like him or not, it is hard to argue that by the time he retired in 2009, Curt Schilling had earned the right to be included amongst the greatest pitchers of all time. In fact, most baseball pundits will agree that he will someday be elected into the Hall of Fame.

During his storied career, Schilling is estimated to have earned nearly $115 million playing the game he loved and millions more through endorsement deals. Yet, by June 2012, Schilling was admittedly broke. What happened? Schilling made a critical mistake that all investors should avoid. He concentrated nearly all of his assets in one investment…and it failed!

Schilling was seemingly as passionate about playing video games as he was about pitching. Plus, he knew the video gaming industry could be very lucrative. To his credit, he developed a plan for his post-baseball career and pursued his dream of building a video gaming business that could rival the best in the business. In 2006, three years before he retired, Schilling launched the company that would eventually come to be known as 38-Studios, which was a tribute to his playing career and the number he wore on his jersey.

Between 2006 and 2012, Schilling is purported to have invested $50 million of his own money into the business, which accounted for most of what remained from his professional baseball earnings. In 2010, 38-Studios also secured a $75 million loan from The Rhode Island Economic Development Corp. to bolster the company's coffers and provide the resources he thought necessary to build the business. Unfortunately for Schilling, his success in the Big Leagues did not translate to success in his business. By mid-2012, it was abundantly clear that Schilling's dream was falling apart. 38-Studios was running out of money, could not pay its 379 employees, and defaulted on loan agreements. The company was liquidated through Chapter 7 bankruptcy[7], with $22 million in assets and nearly $151 million in debt.

---

7 Chapter 7 is a bankruptcy proceeding in which a company stops all operations and goes completely out of business. A trustee is appointed to liquidate (sell) the company's assets, the proceeds are used to pay off the debts, and then the remaining debt is discharged.

Even worse, Schilling declared that he was personally broke. It was a bitter end to such a storied career. The man who had struck out so many batters during the course of his career had suddenly struck out himself. Unfortunately for him, however, it wasn't just a game.

CONDUCTING DUE DILIGENCE

Throughout this book I have stressed the importance of conducting research and due diligence before making an investment. But exactly what does that mean? Broadly defined, due diligence is a comprehensive investigation into the material facts and circumstances of a proposed transaction or investment. Its purpose is to gain a thorough understanding of a proposed investment or transaction and to assess any liabilities and inherent risks.

Admittedly, due diligence is a subjective process. It is more art than science and there is no definitive checklist or approach. It can sometimes be time-consuming, but if conducted properly, brings discipline to an investment process and identifies risks so an investor can make an informed decision. My advice is simple: **Never make an investment without first conducting a reasonable amount of due diligence.**

I generally recommend a phased approach, which brings structure to the process (Figure 6). During each phase, you and your team should analyze the opportunity against a set of criteria designed to eliminate any investment that does not meet your objectives. To be clear, this entire section is likely an over-simplification of what a robust due diligence process would entail. However, the purpose is to provide a broad framework to better help you understand the process. Always consult with an attorney and other financial professionals to determine the breadth and depth of due diligence that should be conducted for a given investment.

Figure 6: Phases of Due Diligence

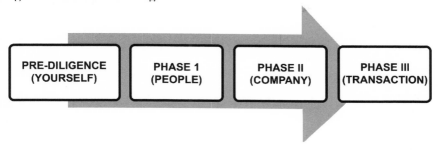

PRE-DILIGENCE: SELF-ASSESSMENT

During the Pre-Diligence Phase, you are effectively performing a self-assessment. Evaluate your financial situation to honestly and candidly determine if the proposed investment is suitable for you, given your unique circumstances and based upon your personal risk tolerance, investment objectives and liquidity needs.

- Have you assessed your net worth? What percentage of your net worth would the proposed investment represent?

- Do you have adequate means and liquidity for providing for your current needs and future obligations and contingencies?

- Are you able to bear the full economic loss of an investment in the company?

- What are your overall investment objectives?

- Have you considered other investment alternatives that may be available? If not, you should consult a financial professional to understand the options available to you.

- What is your risk tolerance? Would you consider yourself a conservative, moderate or aggressive investor?

- Do you have previous experience investing? If so, have you recently evaluated your investment portfolio to determine if you maintain an appropriate mix of assets?

- Is your investment portfolio diversified or concentrated? If you do not know, you should seek counsel from a financial professional.

- Have you built a team of professional advisors who can help you evaluate and analyze the investment opportunity?

- Why are you making the investment? What is your motivation and purpose?

PHASE I: THE PEOPLE

During Phase I, evaluate the experience, integrity and capabilities of the management team and people with whom you are investing. In addition, carefully consider the background of the persons promoting the transaction and the quality of the source introducing you to the investment opportunity.

- What is the background and disciplinary history of the promoter or person recommending the investment opportunity? Do you have a pre-existing personal or business relationship with that person?

- Does the company have an organizational chart for its business?

- Who are the key decision makers?

- What is the compensation of officers and key personnel?

- Consider the experience of the management team, their history of working together and the strength of any references.

- Who are the company's professional advisors?

- Order background checks on key members of the management team.

- Are there any employment contracts or confidentiality agreements?

- What are the current and anticipated staffing needs?

- Does the company have a board of directors or advisory board?

PHASE II: THE COMPANY

During Phase II, you will evaluate the company and its business model, its product offering, growth prospects, industry and target market and the level of competition within the industry.

- Understand the history of the company and any predecessor companies.

- What is the nature of the company's business? Does the company have a business and marketing plan? Do you understand the business model and how the company will make money?

- What products and/or services does the Company offer? What is its value proposition or unique advantage?

- Is there patent, trademark or trade secret protection?

- What are the company's financial needs?

- What are the industry and market dynamics for the company's products and/or services? Is there sufficient demand for the company's product offering? Does the company have existing customers? Does the company operate in a growing market?

- Who are the company's major competitors?

- Does the company have audited financial statements and a robust accounting system?

- Are there any cash flow issues or pending tax problems? Any actual, pending or threatened litigation?

- Are the company's financial projections realistic?

PHASE III: THE TRANSACTION

During Phase III, you will need to evaluate the transaction structure and mechanics to understand your rights and obligations as an investor, expected return on investment, legal protections, tax implications and exit strategy. Understanding the exit strategy is critical because you should know when and under what circumstances, your money will be returned.

- What is the company's corporate and tax status? Is the company in good standing with federal and state authorities and does it have legal authority to enter into the proposed transaction?

- Do you understand the purpose and structure of the transaction? Follow Warren Buffet's advice - NEVER invest in a business or transaction that you do not understand.

- What are the sources and uses of funds for the transaction?

- Is your investment equity or debt? Secured or unsecured? In all cases, you should consult a financial professional to understand your rights and obligations.

- What is the anticipated rate of return?

- When and under what terms will you be repaid? What is your exit strategy?

- What are the tax implications to you for making the investment?

- Are there any regulatory hurdles or approvals required for the investment to be successful? If so, do you understand the requirements and anticipated timing?

- Do you have important investor rights—the right to consult management, access to books and records, the right to receive financial statements, etc.?

- Does the company have any material contracts, indebtedness or real estate holdings that should be considered in connection with the proposed transaction?

- What is the worst-case scenario?

ABOUT THE AUTHOR

Antony has over twenty years of experience as an attorney and investor. He has practiced law domestically and internationally with a leading global law firm and has provided advice and counsel to several professional athletes. He has also worked at a hedge fund with more than $1 billion of assets and served as a member of its Investment Committee.

Antony is a published author whose writings have been featured in the Journal of Investment Management, Fordham's Journal of Corporate & Financial Law and Private Asset Magazine. He has been quoted in Alpha Magazine and Deal Flow Media publications and has been a featured speaker at Cantor Fitzgerald's Hedge Fund Symposium, the M&A Advisors' Distressed Investing Conference and Deal Flow Media's Annual Investing Conference.

Antony earned a Masters of Law (LL.M.) in Securities & Financial Regulation from Georgetown University Law Center, a JD from Howard University School of Law, and a BS in Business Administration with honors from Virginia Union University. Antony is admitted to the Bar in the States of New York and New Jersey and holds FINRA Series 7, 24, 63, 65, 79, 86 and 87 licenses. Antony is also a commissioned officer in the U.S. Army Reserve.

Antony lives with his family in northern New Jersey.

SOURCES

Affinity Fraud

1. Scott Kaminsky, *"Something to Think About: Affinity Fraud – What is it and How Can Professional Athletes Avoid it?"* Access Athletes (June 2, 2013).

2. *"Affinity Fraud – Fleecing the Flock – The big business of swindling people who trust you,"* The Economist (January 8, 2012).

3. *"Affinity Fraud: How to Avoid Investment Scams that Target Groups,"* Securities and Exchange Commission, Investor Publications (October 9, 2013).

4. Matt Krantz, *"Sports stars are naturals for investment scams,"* USA Today (March 19, 2012).

Agents

1. Securities and Exchange Commission, Litigation Release No. 17358, United States v. William H. Black, James A. Franklin, Jr., Alfred Twitty, Linda Wilson and Lisa Adams, No. 1:00CR15 SPM (N.D. Fla.) (February 11, 2000).

2. Securities and Exchange Commission, Litigation Release No. 16455, SEC v. William H. Black, James A. Franklin, Jr., Professional Management, Inc., Professional Management

Consulting, Inc., and Silverline Development Corporation, LLC, No. 8:00CV383-T-26B (M.D. Fla.) (February 25, 2000).

3. Securities and Exchange Commission, Litigation Release No. 17511, United States v. William H. Black, et al., No. 1:00CR15 SPM (N.D. Fla.) (May 8, 2002).

4. Sanchez, Humberto, *"SEC Sues Sports Agency for Defrauding Clients,"* The Wall Street Journal, Feb. 28, 2000.

5. *"After losing everything, Black tells his side of story,"* Pro Sports Group (www.prosportsgroup.com).

6. O'Keefe, Michael, *"Agent of Change,"* New York Daily News (September 12, 2009).

7. Adelson, Eric, *"Ex-NFL running back Fred Taylor forgives former agent who defrauded him of millions,"* Yahoo Sports (August 18, 2012).

Financial Advisors

1. Securities and Exchange Commission, Litigation Release No. 9913, In the Matter of Jeffrey B. Rubin (September 15, 2015).

2. Robbins, Christopher, *"SEC Bars Advisor Who Allegedly Bilked NFL Stars,"* Financial Advisor Magazine (September 16, 2015).

3. FAA Staff, *"Broker Barred from Industry For Bilking NFL Players,"* Financial Advisor Magazine (March 8, 2013).

4. Getlin, Rand, *"Ray Lewis, Frank Gore among group of 16 NFL players suing bank for nearly $53 million,"* Yahoo Sports (October 31, 2013).

5. Jason Cole and Rand Getlin, *"Raucous lifestyle leads to fall of Jeff Rubin, former financial advisor to NFL players,"* Yahoo Sports (September 4, 2012).

6. Cole, Jason, *"$60 million lawsuit points to $100 million scam,"* NFPost. com (October 13, 2013).

7. Garcia-Roberts, Gus, *"Jeff Rubin, T.O.'s Maligned Financial Advisor, Faces Litigation and a Criminal Probe,"* Miami New Times (February 6, 2012).

8. Leonhardt, Megan, *"FINRA Tackles Rep's Bad Advice to Athletes"* (March 8, 2013).

Lawyers

1. Kyle R. Orton, et al. v. Chuhak & Tecson P.C., et al., No. 11 CH 44662.

2. John Flynn Rooney, *"Lawyer faces federal tax fraud charges,"* Chicago Daily Law Bulletin (October 21, 2014).

3. Karen Gullo and Edvard Pettersson, *"NFL's Kyle Orton Sues Chicago Law Firm Over Investments,"* Bloomberg (December 30, 2011).

4. Martha Neil, *"Tax lawyer and DOJ settle suit over claimed $16M shelter scheme; suit by football payers ongoing,"* ABA Journal (November 11, 2013).

5. Jared S. Hopkins, *"Chicago lawyer behind NFL players' tax deals is indicted,"* Chicago Tribune (October 15, 2014).

6. Jared S. Hopkins, *"Feds: Lawyer helped clients claim $16 million in false tax credits,"* Chicago Tribune (November 7, 2013).

7. Lester Munson, *"Green gas, good intent and Kyle Orton,"* ESPN (January 7, 2012).

8. Department of Justice, *"Chicago Lawyer Permanently Barred from Promoting Tax-Fraud Schemes and Preparing Related Tax Returns,"* Justice News - Press Release (November 7, 2013).

9. Glynis Farrell, *"Quarterback Sues Law Firm in Class Action,"* Courthouse News Service (January 3, 2012).

Business Partners

1. Jane Musgrove, *"Zada's $20 million fraud trial starts; NHL star among alleged victims,"* Palm Beach Post (July 27, 2015).

2. Carey Spivak, *"Ponzi con man Joe Zada used the trappings of wealth to lure his victims,"* Journal Sentinel (November 17, 2015).

3. Jane Musgrave, *"Wellington high-flier Zada gets 17 years in prison for $37 million,"* Palm Beach Post (January 23, 2016).

4. Jane Musgrave, *"NHL great Sergei Fedorov testifies he lost $40 million to Zada scheme,"* Palm Beach Post (August 21, 2015).

5. Jane Musgrave, *"Joseph Zada sentenced to more than 17 years in $37 million oil scam,"* Palm Beach Post (January 22, 2016).

6. James O'Brien, *"Sergei Fed3rov's Money Troubles Continue,"* Pro Hockey Talk (July 30, 2015).

Teammates

1. Securities and Exchange Commission v. Capital Financial Partners LLC et al., case number 1:15-cv-11447, (D. Mass).

2. United States of America v. Will D. Allen and Susan C. Daub, Case No. 15-mj-7095-JCB (D. Mass.).

3. U.S. Securities and Exchange Commission, Litigation Release No. 23286 (June 15, 2015).

4. U.S. Securities and Exchange Commission, Litigation Release No. 23232 (April 7, 2013).

5. Jeff Ostrowski, *"Former Dolphin Will Allen: New twist on pro athletes in poor house?"* Palm Beach Post (July 24, 2015).

6. Rafael Olmeda, *"Ex-Dolphins player faces charges in Ponzi scheme,"* Fort Lauderdale News (June 12, 2015).

7. Alex Hinz, *"SEC v. Capital Financial Partners LLC – Complaint,"* www.theracetothebottom.org (August 6, 2015).

Family and Friends

1. Corey Howard v. RJH Enterprises, LLC, Case 4:13-cv-02518-CEJ (Filed: 12/18/13).

2. Matt Snyder, *"Ryan Howard recently finished legal battle with family over money,"* www.cbssports.com (November 19, 2014).

3. Matt Lombardo, *"Phillies' Ryan Howard involved in bitter lawsuit with family over his finances,"* www.nj.com (November 19,2014).

4. David Murphy, *"The family legal fight over Ryan Howard's finances,"* www.philly.com (November 19, 2014).

5. Matt Gelb, *"Money issues tear at Ryan Howard and his family,"* www.philly.com (November 21, 2014.

6. Scott Butler, *"Details of Ryan Howard lawsuit more than disturbing,"* www.philsbaseball.com (November 22, 2014).

7. Glenn Minnis, *"Ryan Howard Reaches Settlement In Nasty Fraud Suit Involving Family Members,"* www.business2community.com (November 25, 2014).

Unauthorized Investments

1. Securities and Exchange Commission v. Louis Martin Blazer III, ECF Case 16-CV-03384 (May 6, 2016).

2. SEC Press Release 2016-83, *"SEC: Financial Advisor Defrauded Pro Athletes and Lied to SEC Examiners,"* (May 6, 2016).

3. SEC Litigation Release No. 23534 (S.D.N.Y. May 6, 2016).

4. Matthew Heller, *"Financial Adviser Accused of Stealing $2.3M,"* www.cfo.com/us May 6, 2016).

5. Karen Demasters, *"Pittsburgh Advisor Cheated Professional Athletes, SEC Says,"* Financial Advisor Magazine (May 6, 2016).

6. Alex Nixon and David Conti, *"Ex-financial adviser accused of running a ponzi-scheme with pro athletes' money,"* www.triblive.com (May 6, 2016).

Unsuitable Investments

1. Adam Joshua Feely; Heather Mitts; Brent Celek; and Kevin Curtis v. SunTrust Bank, Inc.; Martin Kelly Capital Management, LLC; William Crafton, Jr.; CSI Capital Management, Inc.; John Does 1-50, U.S. District Court for the Eastern District of Pennsylvania, Complaint and Jury Demand.

2. SEC v. Westmoore Management, LLC et al, USDC N. SACV10-00849 AG (MLX) (June 15, 2010).

3. Securities and Exchange Commission v. Bill C. (Billy) Crafton, Civil Action No. 3:14-cv-02916-DMS-JLB, Litigation Release No. 23155 (December 11, 2014).

4. Securities and Exchange Commission, In the Matter of Bill C. (Billy) Crafton, Jr., Order Instituting Administrative Proceedings Pursuant to Section 15(b) of the Securities Exchange Act of

1934 and Section 203(f) of the Investment Advisors Act of 1940, Making Findings, and Imposing Remedial Sanctions.

5. Investment Advisor Representative Public Disclosure Report, Bill Clay Crafton Jr., CRD #4018081, Report #59482-11463 (as of January 12, 2015).

6. Matthias Riker, *"SEC Orders Former Advisor to NFL Players to Pay $1.7 Million,"* The Wall Street Journal (December 11, 2014).

7. Don Bauder, *"Shell Game for Athletes,"* San Diego Reader (October 23, 2013).

8. Don Bauder, *"FBI sting nabs sports agents plotting to screw clients,"* San Diego Reader (January 22, 2015).

9. Don Bauder, *"Government nabs jock swindler,"* San Diego Reader (December 12, 2014).

Misrepresentation

1. Andrew Goodman, *"The Ponzi Scheme You've Never Heard of that Cost NFL, NBA Players Millions,"* Forbes (June 27, 2013).

2. U.S. Securities and Exchange Commission, Administrative Proceeding – File No. 3-16755, In the Matter of Success Trade, Inc., Success Trade Securities, Inc. and Fuad Ahmed (December 21, 2015).

3. Michael Leibel, *"U.S. Brokerage Must Pay Athletes $13.7 Million for Ponzi Fraud: FINRA,"* Financial Advisor Magazine (June 26, 2014).

4. Dina ElBoghdady, *"Regulators accuse Success Trade Securities owner of scamming NFL, NBA players,"* The Washington Post (April 11, 2013).

5. Pete Brush, *"Success Trade to Pay $27M to Settle SEC Ponzi Allegations,"* Law360 (August 17, 2015).

Misappropriation

1. U.S. Securities and Exchange Commission, Litigation Release No. 19581, (February 28, 2006).

2. Securities and Exchange Commission v. Kirk S. Wright, et al, Civil Action No. 1:06-CV-0438 (NDGA February 27, 2006).

3. Ian McDonald and Valerie Bauerlein, *"Troubles at Atlanta Hedge Fund Snare Doctors, Football Players,"* The Wall Street Journal (March 9, 2006).

4. Carl Horowitz, *"Circuit Court Sides with NFL, Players Union in Fraud Suit,"* National Legal and Policy Center (February 28, 2011).

5. Ann Brown, *"A Tale of Caution,"* Black Enterprise (June 6, 2008).

6. Mike Tierney, *"Hedge Fund Manager's Death Does Not Halt Suit Against NFL and Players Union,"* (June 2, 2008).

Ponzi Scheme

1. The People of the State of Colorado v. Sean Michael Mueller,

District Court, City and County of Denver, Colorado, Case Number 10CR10319 (October 12, 2010).

2. Greg Griffin, *"Ponzi-schemer Sean Mueller gets 40-year prison sentence,"* Denver Post (December 6, 2010).

3. Al Lewis, *"Alleged Ponzi in Colorado Has Shades of Madoff Affair,"* The Wall Street Journal (April 29, 2010).

4. Paul Sullivan, *"How to Avoid Being Taken in by a Ponzi Scheme,"* The New York Times (December 10, 2010).

5. *"NFL Quarterback John Elway Victim of Ponzi Scheme,"* The Legal Examiner (October 17, 2010).

6. *"Don't Get Sacked with Investment Fraud,"* Protect Your Pocket Series, Indiana Securities Division (Originally published October 2010).

Pump-and-Dump

1. Press Release, *"SEC Charges Daniel "Rudy" Ruettiger and 12 Others in Scheme to Pump Stock in Sports Drink Company,"* Securities and Exchange Commission (December 16, 2011).

2. U.S. Securities and Exchange Commission, Litigation Release No. 22198 (December 16, 2011).

Other

1. Applied Research and Consulting LLC, prepared for the FINRA Financial Education Foundation, *"Financial Fraud and Fraud Susceptibility in the United States,"* Research Report from a 2012 National Survey" (September 2013).

INDEX